Personal, Moral, So... and Cultural education

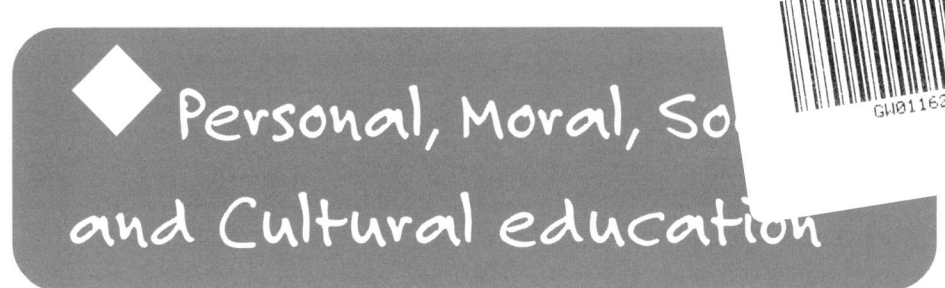

GROWING UP TODAY
Looking after ourselves

Key Stage 1/P1–3

Ros Bayley and Lynn Broadbent

HOPSCOTCH EDUCATIONAL PUBLISHING

Acknowledgements

Published by Hopscotch Educational Publishing Company Ltd,
29 Waterloo Place, Leamington Spa CV32 5LA 01926 744227

© 1999 Hopscotch Educational Publishing

Written by Ros Bayley and Lynn Broadbent
Cover design by Kim Ashby
Page design by Steve Williams
Illustrated by Cathy Gilligan
Cover illustration by Cathy Gilligan
Printed by Clintplan, Southam

Ros Bayley and Lynn Broadbent hereby assert their moral right to be identified as the authors of this work in accordance with the Copyright, Designs and Patents Act, 1988.

ISBN 1-902239-20-2

All rights reserved. This book is sold subject to the condition that it shall not, by way of trade or otherwise, be lent, hired out or otherwise circulated without the publisher's prior consent in any form or binding or cover other than that in which it is published and without a similar condition, including this condition, being imposed upon the subsequent purchaser.

No part of this publication may be reproduced, stored in a retrieval system, or transmitted, in any form or by any means, electronic, mechanical photocopying, recording or otherwise, without the prior permission of the publisher, except where photocopying for educational purposes within the school or other educational establishment that has purchased this book is expressly permitted in the text.

Contents

Introduction	4
Health and hygiene	6
Drugs and our health	11
Personal safety	16
Healthy eating	21
Water safety	26
Standing up for ourselves	31
Keeping safe at home	36
Road safety	41
Generic sheets	
Charlie and the bag	46
Looking after ourselves	47

Introduction

Broadly speaking 'Looking after ourselves' is about health education. The focus books that have been selected cover a diverse range of issues and have been chosen to enable teachers and children to explore areas like road safety, healthy eating, water safety and personal hygiene. We have also included more complex issues such as drug education and personal safety and, in using the story 'Pay Up, Or Else!' we have offered a vehicle through which personal empowerment and bullying may be explored.

It is our intention that the chapters that follow can be used to support children's health education in Key Stage 1/P1-3. Most importantly we feel that every book in the 'Growing Up Today' series has a significant contribution to make in terms of helping children make health promoting choices.

Health education is complex. It is about so much more than how to wash our hands and clean our teeth properly. If we are to succeed in our health education programmes it is essential that we understand those complexities and provide children with an integrated programme of work that promotes a healthy lifestyle.

In addition to providing children with information we need to develop their sense of responsibility, their decision-making skills and their ability to think reflectively. If children are to make positive choices it is necessary that they possess good expressive and communicating skills. It is also crucial that they are able to value themselves and others, know about making choices and understand the ways in which these choices can impact on their lives.

We are living in a society that has undergone unprecedented change. The task for us as adults is to help children gain the skills, knowledge and attitudes that will enable them to cope with an ever-increasing range of choices. It would also seem important that we help children to understand that we will not always make the right choices and consider what we might do in response to making a 'wrong' choice.

In short, we will not be effective in our health education programmes, if we fail to take full account of children's emotional education.

They need to be able to understand and process their feelings and know which feelings they can trust. They need to know whom they can trust and confide in, and who they cannot. Risk assessment is also important, and not always easy, for when things are safe and when they are not can vary.

The more we reflect upon health education the more apparent its complexities become and it is for this reason we would like you to consider the whole of the 'Growing Up Today' series as important to health education.

BIBLIOGRAPHY OF TITLES REFERRED TO IN THIS BOOK

Doctor Dog by Babette Cole (Red Fox, Random House Books)

Nice or Nasty: Learning About Drugs and Your Health by Claire Llewellyn (Wayland)

Mummy, Mummy, Where Are You? by Ann de Bode and Rien Broere (Evans Brothers)

The Food We Eat by Paul Humphrey (Evans Brothers)

Look Out By Water by Helena Ramsay (Evans Brothers)

Pay Up, Or Else! by Ann de Bode (Evans Brothers)

Look Out at Home by Helena Ramsay (Evans Brothers)

Take Care on the Road by Carole Wale (Wayland)

Health and hygiene

FOCUS BOOK

DOCTOR DOG
by Babette Cole
Red Fox, Random
House Books

INTENDED LEARNING

◆ To enhance the children's understanding of the importance of some simple hygiene rules.
◆ To extend the children's knowledge of cause and effect with regard to some common complaints.

Synopsis of the story

'Doctor Dog' is at a medical conference in Brazil but has to return home when the Gumboyle family become ill. Not only is he the family pet, he is also their personal physician. Whatever the problem, Dr Dog is on hand to offer sound advice and appropriate treatment. Sadly, the Gumboyle family, who do not always do the necessary things to ensure a healthy life style, wear him out to the extent that poor Dr Dog needs a holiday to help him to recover. Unfortunately, the family miss him so much that they fly out to join him!

Notes for teachers

This book is full of both sound advice and good fun, most of which is due to the everso-slightly rude bits! Children don't always see the connection between the things they are asked to do and the possible consequences of not doing them. This is a book about cause and effect and really helps young children to understand the reasons for observing simple hygienic practices. Sound advice is presented in an amusing and memorable way and will be far more effective in getting over the importance of basic hygiene than all the nagging in the world.

'Doctor Dog' is an excellent book to use at anytime, but it may prove particularly useful at specific times, for example should there be an outbreak of nits or worms in the school. Either way, the children will really enjoy health education presented in this novel and everso-slightly naughty way!

Methodology

◆ Although this is a very humorous book it deals with some important health education issues, the first of which is smoking. You could begin by asking the children: Kurt Gumboyle had a bad cough because he had been smoking. What did Dr Dog say would happen to his lungs if he kept smoking? It may be helpful to get the children to take a deep breath and relate the process of breathing to the picture of the lungs. Get them to identify where their lungs are in their bodies. You might take in a packet of cigarettes and point out the health warning on the side of the packet. Ask: What do you know about smoking? What diseases can it cause?

◆ Like Gertie Gumboyle, everyone gets a cold from time to time but it might be worth asking the children: Can we help prevent colds by keeping ourselves warm and dry? Do you know why this is? (Being cold lowers our resistance to viruses.)

◆ Kev Gumboyle gets nits, which provides us with an opportunity for discussing what can sometimes be a sensitive issue. Ask: Do you know what nits are? What are some of the ways in which we can get nits? Is there anything we can do to protect ourselves from nits? If you do get nits, what do you have to do to get rid of them? It might be helpful to take in some lotion, such as tea-tree oil, and a toothcomb to help the children to see how the nits and the lice can be killed and combed from the hair.

◆ Baby Gumboyle gets worms and this part of the story is excellent for helping the children to understand the importance of not sucking their fingers, and washing their hands after they've been to the toilet. Ask them: How do you think Baby Gumboyle got worms? What happened when he scratched his bottom? Show the children the picture of the magnifying glass and the thumb. Ask: What does the picture tell us about worms?

◆ Fiona Gumboyle suffers from dizziness as a consequence of earache. Ask: Why can having earache make us feel dizzy? It may help the children to understand this if they can look at a poster or 3D model of the inner ear.

◆ To help them to appreciate the connection between diet and the digestive system, ask: Why did Grandad Gumboyle get terrible wind? If the children have done any work on the digestive system they may know that some foods create more gases in the body than others. If not, this may need some explanation. Good luck!

The photocopiable activity sheets

Find the connection This activity is intended for children who may not yet be recording formally. It requires them to think about the cause and effect in relation to health and hygiene.

What happens when...? As with the previous activity the children are asked to link cause with effect and present their answers as drawings.

Peter's day This activity is also about cause and effect but is intended for children who can write independently.

FURTHER READING

Why Wash? Learning About Personal Hygiene by Claire Llewellyn (Wayland)

◆ Find the connection ◆

◆ Cut out these pictures and match the cause to the effect.

What happens when...?

◆ Draw pictures to show what can happen when...

Peter's day

◆ Write some sentences to tell Peter what would happen if he does not look after his body.

At 8 o'clock Peter refuses to clean his teeth.

At 10.30 Peter won't wash his hands after going to the toilet.

_____

_____

At noon Peter eats some sweets but throws his sandwiches and fruit away.

At 9 o'clock at night Peter goes to bed without having a wash.

_____

_____

Drugs and our health

FOCUS BOOK

NICE OR NASTY: LEARNING ABOUT DRUGS AND YOUR HEALTH
by Claire Llewellyn
Wayland

INTENDED LEARNING

◆ To help deliver the key messages about drugs identified in the notes for teachers.

Synopsis of the text

Presented in an accessible cartoon style this book deals with the safe use of medicines and other substances in the home. It helps children understand that whilst all medicines are drugs, not all drugs are medicines. It warns of the dangers of such drugs and how they can damage our health if misused. This is a non-fiction text which many children will be able to read for themselves. It also contains an index, a simple glossary and suggestions for further reading, and as such is excellent for supporting work with literacy.

Notes for teachers

It is not unusual for teachers to feel some apprehension about tackling drug education, but as long as we are 'starting from where the children are' and making the work age appropriate there is little to fear. In order to find out 'where the children are' in their understanding of drugs it is a good idea to begin this piece of work with a simple draw-and-write exercise (you will find one on page 46 at the back of this book). This will clarify exactly what the children already know and you will know exactly what you are dealing with.

It is essential that we understand what constitutes key messages about drugs for children in Key Stage 1/P1–3. It is important that they learn:
◆ what goes into our body;
◆ about medicines, pills and injections;
◆ about when to say 'No';
◆ about where we might find things that are not safe to touch, taste or sniff;
◆ about the things which can harm us, for example, tobacco, smoke, sprays, liquids and drinks;
◆ about whom we can trust and confide in;
◆ where and how we obtain medicines;
◆ that some drugs prevent us from contracting disease;
◆ that some people have to take medicine every day in order to live a 'normal life';
◆ when things are safe and when they are not, and this will vary.

Methodology

◆ Share pages 4-7 with the children and ask: Can you think of a time when you have had medicine from the doctor? What was it for? How did it help you?

◆ Pages 8 and 9 deal with conditions that need constant medication. Ask: Do you know anybody who has to take medicine every day? How does the medicine help them?

◆ Pages 10-21 deal with drugs as medicines and emphasises the need to treat them with respect. Once you have shared these pages with the children, clarify their understanding by asking: Why do you think babies have injections? Can we buy ANY medicines from the chemist? Why should we never take anyone else's medicine?

◆ Pages 22-23 deal with alcohol and tobacco. Ask: What happens to people if they smoke a lot of tobacco? What can happen if people drink too much alcohol?

◆ Pages 24 and 25 deal with other dangerous substances. Ask: Can you think of anything else around the home that could be harmful? It maybe useful to look at the warning symbols on a collection of products.

◆ On pages 26 and 27 the misuse of drugs is introduced. Whilst the text suggests alcohol and tobacco, the children may begin to mention other drugs. If this happens, accept what they have to say in a matter-of-fact way as possible, continuing to put across the key messages identified in the notes for teachers.

The concluding message is about the need to acknowledge that our bodies are precious and how we should take responsibility for looking after them.
N.B. The task for us as adults is to help children deal with an ever-increasing range of choices. This will require them to have good expressive and communication skills and a high degree of self-awareness. The first three books in the Growing Up Today series will help and support the development of these skills.

The photocopiable activity sheets

Things that contain drugs The activity is about speaking, listening and discussion. It asks the children to think about things that contain drugs but does not require a written response.

Medicines and drugs For this activity the children are asked to think about the distinction between drugs that are medicines and drugs that are not medicines. Again, no writing is involved.

Good or bad for you? This activity sheet builds on the previous one by asking the children to think about ways in which drugs are used. It is designed for children who can write independently. However for those children who are not ready a scribe could be used.

Things that contain drugs

◆ Look at the pictures. Circle the things you think contain drugs.

◆ Compare your answers with your friends.
Talk about any differences.

Hopscotch ◆ Looking after ourselves KS1/P1–3   PHOTOCOPIABLE PAGE   13

◆ Medicines and drugs ◆

All medicines are drugs but not all drugs are medicines.

◆ Look carefully at the pictures. Cut them out and put them into two groups:
Group 1 – Drugs that are medicines
Group 2 – Drugs that are not medicines

◆ Good or bad for you? ◆

◆ Work with some friends and talk about these two questions. Write your thoughts in the boxes.

1. Can drugs be good for you? If so, when?

2. Can drugs be bad for you? If so, when?

Hopscotch ◆ Looking after ourselves KS1/P1–3   PHOTOCOPIABLE PAGE   15

◆Personal safety

FOCUS BOOK

MUMMY, MUMMY, WHERE ARE YOU?
by Ann de Bode and
Rien Broere
Evans Brothers

INTENDED LEARNING

◆ To enhance the children's understanding of how they might most sensibly respond to finding themselves lost in a large busy place.

Synopsis of the story

This story takes place in a large department store where Jessie is shopping with her mum. As she becomes increasingly bored she decides to hide. Unfortunately, she hides so well that by the time she is fed up with the game she cannot find her mum anywhere. At first she is quite calm, but as time goes on she begins to panic and when a stranger taps her on the shoulder and offers to help her she runs out of the store into the busy street. It doesn't take long for her to realise that not only has she lost her mum, she has lost her way as well. Fortunately, she spots a security guard who takes her into a store and telephones around the other stores until Jessie's mum is found.

Notes for teachers

Most young children have experienced being lost at one time or another and when this happens to them they are left feeling frightened and vulnerable. Being lost is bad enough in itself, but the situation can be even more alarming if you are powerless to know how to deal with things. 'Mummy, Mummy, Where Are You?' helps children explore issues around being lost. They can think about and internalise important information about how to respond to finding themselves lost and alone in a vast space. Young children are natural explorers and when out shopping with adults who have a very specific agenda, may frequently seek compensation by exploring their surroundings. When this happens they can easily become lost, and it is at this point that they need to know what to do. The story also enables us to explore 'stranger danger' and road safety issues.

Methodology

When they have listened to this story many children will be anxious to share their own experiences of being lost. Once they have done this they will be better able to concentrate on the issues raised by the story.

- It is important for them to understand the conflicting interests of Jessie and her mother. Show them the picture on page 9 and ask: How does Jessie feel and what does she want? Why do you think mum is pulling her away from the escalator?
- The children will easily relate to Jessie's boredom. Ask: Is there anything else Jessie could have done to amuse herself while her mum was shopping?
- To help the children understand Jessie's rising panic get them to explore her facial expressions. Ask: Can you think of words to describe Jessie's feelings?
- As the story progresses Jessie experiences a wide range of feelings. Introduce some new feelings words, such as exhilarated, frustrated, confused, embarrassed and petrified. Ask: When do you think Jessie is most petrified?
- Jessie ran away when the stranger tapped her on the shoulder. Ask: Why did Jessie run away? Should she have accepted the stranger's offer of help? This question needs to be handled with great care as what we seek to communicate is the uncertainty of the situation. The stranger might have wanted to be genuinely helpful, but on the other hand, he might not.
- Jessie ran out of the store. Ask: Was this a sensible thing to do? What might have happened to Jessie?
- Jessie saw a security guard and assumed he was a policeman. Ask: Are all men in uniform safe?
- Recap on what the security guard did to find Jessie's mum. Ask the children: If this happened to you what would you need to tell the security guard?
- Encourage the children to think about mum's feelings. Ask them: While Jessie was lost, what do you think her mum was doing? Why did her mum have tears in her eyes when she found Jessie?
- Get the children to think about a time when they were lost and ask: Were your parents angry with you? Why do you think they were angry?
- Jessie says she will not get lost again. Ask: Can Jessie be sure that this will never happen? What should she do if she does get lost again?

The photocopiable activity sheets

Who can help? This activity sheet is intended for children who are not yet writing independently. It asks them to think about who could help them if they were lost. (There is no right or wrong answer here.)

Getting help! Children who are not yet writing independently will need help with this. They have to write their name, address and telephone number.

Can you help? This would benefit from some support such as a class discussion. It is for children who can write independently.

Hopscotch ◆ Looking after ourselves KS1/P1–3

◆ Who can help? ◆

◆ Look at these people. Put a ✔ by those people who you could ask for help if you were lost.

◆ Draw a picture of someone who would help you if you were lost.

◆ Getting help! ◆

◆ Imagine that you are lost in this busy shop.
Draw yourself in the picture.

◆ Now write the information that the security guard will need to have in order to help you.

Your name _____

Your address _____

_____

_____

Your telephone number _____

Hopscotch ◆ Looking after ourselves KS1/P1–3   PHOTOCOPIABLE PAGE   19

Can you help?

◆ Look at this picture of a little boy who is lost.

◆ Write one list of the things the little boy should do and another list of the things he should not do.

DO	DON'T

◆ Healthy eating

FOCUS BOOK

THE FOOD WE EAT
by Pat Humphrey
Evans Brothers

INTENDED LEARNING

◆ To enhance the children's understanding of the importance of eating a balanced diet and increase their knowledge of how this may be achieved.

Synopsis of the story

This text takes the form of a first information book that many children will be able to read for themselves. It combines drawings with photographs of foods and is attractively presented. Two children discuss with their mother the issue of which foods are good for them. The focus is on eating a balanced diet and much of the text revolves around how this can be done. The book then goes on to look at how foods are produced and where they come from.

Notes for teachers

Many of us like to eat too much of the things that are not necessarily good for us, but the reassuring thing about this text is the way in which it focuses on eating a 'balanced' diet. The book begins refreshingly with the children enjoying biscuits and the issue is around not eating too many rather than not eating them at all. This book is about making healthy choices and is not a list of do's and don'ts.

'The Food We Eat' is an excellent springboard into work on healthy eating but before sharing it with the children it is helpful to collect a few simple resources, such as other books about food and diet, a collection of tins, packets and fresh food products from a variety of countries and cultures, and globes and maps. It is also important to be aware of the cultural and religious issues associated with food and to check this with parents and carers prior to commencing the work.

The book does not go into the connection between food intake and exercise, therefore it would be beneficial to carry out some additional work on this aspect of health education.

Hopscotch ◆ Looking after ourselves KS1/P1–3

Methodology

◆ The book begins by telling us that it is not good to eat too many sweet things. Ask the children: Why is it not good for us to eat too many sweet things?
◆ The children's mother explains the importance of eating a balanced diet. Ask: What is meant by a 'balanced' diet? Why is it important to eat a balanced diet? What sort of things does a balanced diet contain?
◆ Pages 8 and 9 deal with carbohydrates. Ask: Why should we eat carbohydrates? What type of foods contain carbohydrates? (This is when it is useful to have a collection of real foods. The children can then pick out the things that fit into this food type.)
◆ Pages 10 and 11 talk about proteins. Ask: Why is it important to eat enough protein? Which foods contain protein? (The text does not refer to dairy products or pulses as sources of protein so you will need to tell the children about them.)
◆ Pages 12 and 13 deal with vitamins. Ask: Which types of food contain vitamins? Why are vitamins important to our health?
◆ The remaining pages deal with how food is produced and where it comes from. It may be useful to ask the following questions:
  - Why is wheat important as a food?
  - How many foods can you think of that will contain wheat?
  - Why is rice important as a food?
  - What do we mean when we talk about dairy products?
  - In what sort of ways can we buy fish?
  - Can you think of the sorts of fruit and vegetables that can be grown in this country?
  - What sort of fruit and vegetables cannot be grown in this country?
  - Why is it important for us to think carefully about the things that we eat?
  - What do you think can happen to our bodies if we don't eat a balanced diet?
◆ It is profitable to get the children to think about their own diets. Ask: Which foods do you like to eat most? Do you think you eat a balanced diet? How do you get your protein/carbohydrates/vitamins? Do you think you eat too much or too little of any type of food?
◆ Ask the children to keep a diary of what they have eaten over a period of several days and evaluate how nutritious and balanced their food intake has been.

The photocopiable activity sheets

A balanced meal This activity asks the children to apply what they have learned about nutrition by designing a balanced meal.

Different types of food For this cut-and-paste activity the children have to classify foods into groups.

Healthy meals This is intended for children who can write independently and involves thinking and reasoning skills.

◆ A balanced meal ◆

◆ Think about a meal you would enjoy. Make sure it is a balanced meal. Draw the things you would eat.

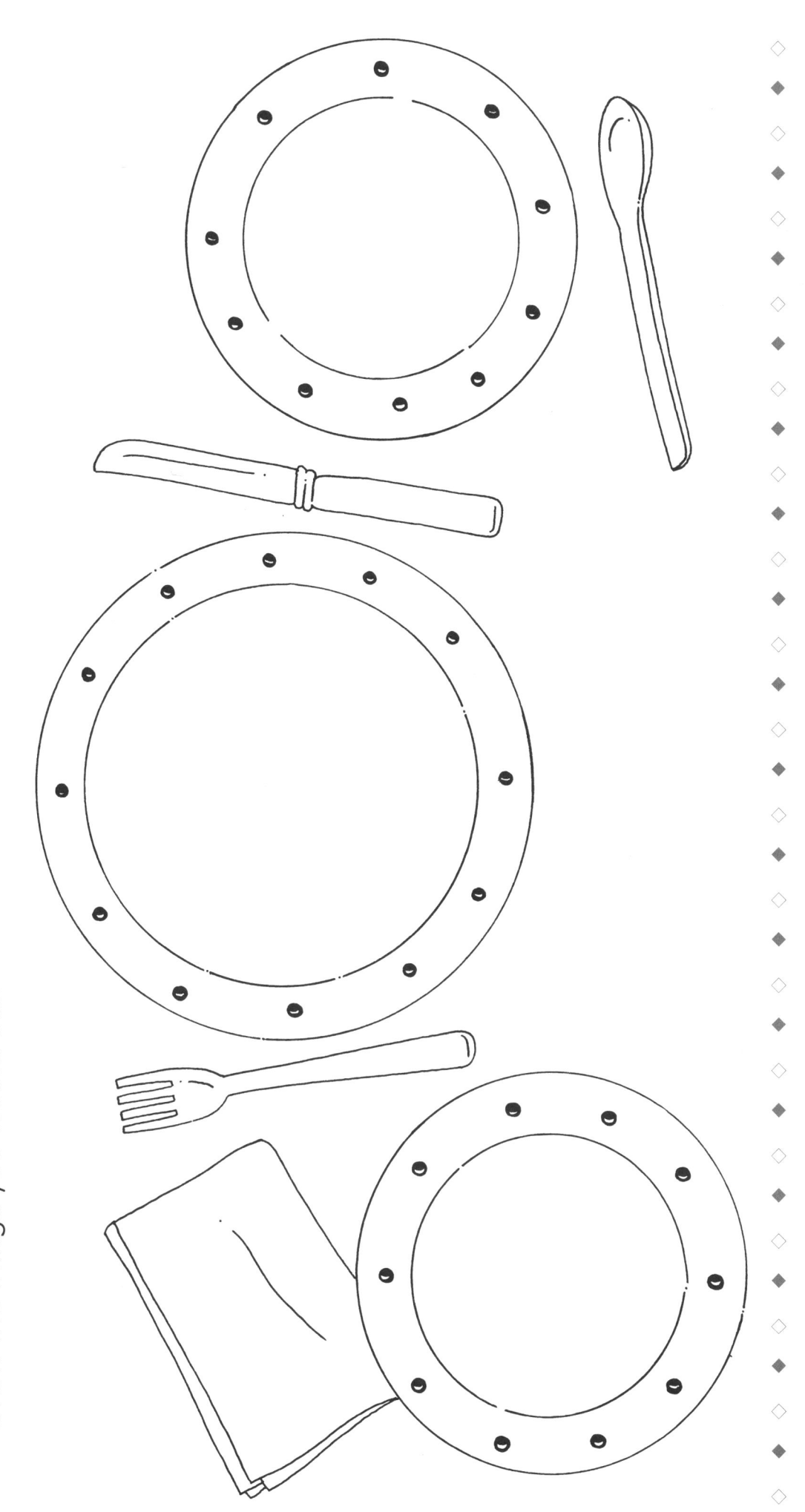

Hopscotch ◆ Looking after ourselves KS1/P1–3   PHOTOCOPIABLE PAGE

◆ Different types of food ◆

◆ Look at the pictures of food below. Cut them out and put them in the right box.

Food with lots of protein	Food with lots of carbohydrate
Food with lots of vitamins	Food with lots of fats and sugar

PHOTOCOPIABLE PAGE

Hopscotch ◆ Looking after ourselves KS1/P1–3

◆ Healthy meals ◆

◆ Look at these two meals. Put a ✔ by the one that is the most balanced.

◆ Give your reasons for why we should eat the most balanced meal more often than the other one.

_____
_____
_____
_____
_____
_____
_____

Water safety

FOCUS BOOK

LOOK OUT BY WATER
by Helena Ramsay
Evans Brothers

INTENDED LEARNING

◆ To heighten the children's awareness of the dangers associated with playing near water. To generate strategies and rules to help them keep safe by water.

Synopsis of the story

'Look out by Water' is a simple non-fiction text which many children will be able to read independently. It deals with the various hazards that can be encountered at the seaside and the swimming baths and touches briefly on lakes and rivers. It does not, however, make any reference to canals, so for children living in areas where there is a canal network it is important to stress that many of the hazards mentioned can apply when walking or playing near canals. The book is an attractive combination of drawings and photographs and provides a good foundation for work on water safety.

Notes for teachers

This text has been compiled in consultation with RoSPA (Royal Society for the Prevention of Accidents) and is full of sound advice. Many children are killed or injured each year as a result of accidents by water; accidents that may well have been avoided had the children concerned had a greater awareness of how to stay safe when playing in or around water. By sharing this text with the children we can provide opportunities for them to generate a water safety code and gain important knowledge that may one day help to keep them safe.

When using this book it is also useful to have a collection of additional non-fiction material relating to rivers, lakes, canals and the seaside.

Methodology

As much of this text focuses on the seaside it may be worth checking to see if there are any children who have never been to the seaside. If there are, some extra support and clarification may be necessary.

◆ Pages 4 and 5 stress the importance of never playing near water unless accompanied by an adult. Ask the children the following questions:
  - Why do you think the book tells us that we should always have an adult with us when playing by water?
  - Why is it important to walk at the swimming baths or when moving around on rocks?
  - Can you think of any other important rules to help keep us safe when near water?
  - What do we need to know before we jump into water?
  - Why is it important to know the depth of the water?
  - Why is it important to find a safe place to get into the water?
  - Can you name some safe places?

◆ The book tells us that the water at the seaside can become deeper very quickly. Ask: Why do you think this happens? How is the seabed different from the bottom of a swimming pool?

◆ Pages 19 to 21 talk about currents. Ask: What is meant by a strong current and what can happen if you get caught in one? Where else might you find a current?

◆ Pages 22 and 23 talk about tides. For some children this may need further explanation. Ask: The book warns us about getting 'cut off by the tide'. What does it mean by this?

◆ The final six pages deal with safety when on a boat. Ask: Why is it important to wear a life jacket even if you can swim? Why is it important to sit down on a boat? Why are we told that we should not lean over the sides?

◆ Although the text deals with the most common dangers associated with water there is still room for some further exploration, and it is worth getting the children to think about other potentially dangerous situations. Ask: Can you think of any other places where there is water and where we may need to be especially careful? (Ponds in fields, streams, brooks, lakes in the park.)

The photocopiable activity sheets

Keeping safe by water This is a sorting activity requiring careful observational and thinking skills. The children have to think which children in the picture are behaving sensibly and which are not. There is no writing involved.

Danger! This sheet has a similar objective to the first one but requires a small amount of written recording.

Help them to keep safe For this activity the children are asked to apply their learning by compiling a 'safety' list. It is intended for children who can write independently.

FURTHER READING

Take Care Near Water by Carole Wale (Wayland)

Keeping safe by water

◆ Some of these children are being very sensible but some are not.
Put a ✔ by the pictures where the children are sensible.
Put a ✘ by the pictures where they are not.

◆ Danger! ◆

◆ Look carefully at this picture. Put a red ✖ by the children who could be in danger. Compare your answers with a friend.

◆ Write a sentence to say how you would keep safe at the seaside.

_____

_____

_____

Hopscotch ◆ Looking after ourselves KS1/P1–3   PHOTOCOPIABLE PAGE

◆ Help them to keep safe ◆

◆ These two children are going on holiday to the seaside.

◆ Make a list of all the important things they will need to know if they are to keep safe by the water.

_____
_____
_____
_____
_____
_____
_____
_____
_____

Standing up for ourselves

FOCUS BOOK

PAY UP, OR ELSE!
by Ann de Bode
Evans Brothers

INTENDED LEARNING

◆ To enhance the children's understanding of the ways in which they might support themselves should they become victims of bullying or abusive behaviour by their peers.

Synopsis of the story

This is a story about how a young boy deals with a gang who are running a 'protection racket' in his school. Robert, the main character, is worried about his friend Philip who seems to be behaving very strangely. The whole school is afraid of the gang and Philip becomes one of their victims and has to steal things for them. When they take his silver pen he pretends that it has been stolen. The teacher warns the class that there is a thief among them. Robert decides to try and catch the thief but is faced with a considerable moral dilemma when he sees his friend going through people's pockets. Should he tell the teacher? Although he doesn't fully understand what is going on he eventually confides in his teacher and the gang is punished.

Notes for teachers

It is not uncommon for young children to find themselves the victim of a gang that picks on them and exploits them. When this happens it can have a devastating effect on their lives. Children who have previously been happy and secure can suddenly start to behave very strangely. They may try everything to avoid having to attend school and spend their time preoccupied with worrying about what will happen next. Too frightened about what the gang might do to them, they endure tremendous misery rather than seek help.

If we suspect that a child is being abused in this way, we should give the matter our most serious consideration. In 'Pay Up, Or Else!' the children are listened to and supported by sensitive adults. Robert is confident that he can confide in his teacher and the situation is taken very seriously. By sharing this book with children we can help them to understand how they might respond if they or their friends find themselves in similar circumstances.

Methodology

♦ Sharing this story with children requires us to exercise great sensitivity. It would be inappropriate to encourage children to share their personal experiences in an open forum. Should they offer such information we need to handle the situation extremely carefully as such disclosures can put children in a very vulnerable position.

♦ The story revolves around some very powerful feelings and is an excellent opportunity to extend children's emotional education. Ask: How did Robert feel about the way his friend was behaving? Why do you think the gang picked on Philip? Would it have been as easy to pick on Robert?

♦ Clarify their understanding of the situation by asking: What were the gang making Philip do? How do you think Philip was feeling? Why was Robert so anxious to do something about the situation?

♦ Use various illustrations to help the children to understand Robert's confusion. Ask the following questions:
  - What do you think is happening here?
  - What does Robert think is happening?
  - How does Robert feel when he sees Philip going through the coat pockets?
  - How did Robert feel about telling the teacher? Do you think he found this easy?
  - Why did Robert feel relieved and then feel like crying? What might he be afraid of?
  - What do you think Robert could have done if the teacher had not listened to him? Could he have gone to anyone else for help?

♦ Discuss the children's ideas about what should happen to the gang. Ask:
  - What do you think the Headteacher said to the gang?
  - What do you think should happen to them?
  - Do you think Philip will have any more problems with the gang?
  - If the gang picks on Philip again, what do you think he should do about it?

♦ Help the children to explore peer issues. Ask them: Why do you think some children form gangs? What would you do if someone asked you to join a gang?

♦ It is really important for the children to understand why they should always seek help in such situations. Ask: If the same thing happened to you as happened to Philip, who could you go to for help?

The photocopiable activity sheets

Who would you tell? This activity asks the children to think about who they would confide in if they were being bullied. They record answers through drawings.

What would you do? This sheet will involve speaking, listening and discussion around how children might respond to being bullied. It involves no writing.

Can you help? If the children are to do this activity successfully it should be preceded by much discussion. It asks them to think about how they could support someone who is being bullied. It is for independent writers.

◆ Who would you tell? ◆

◆ If you are being picked on by other children it is important to tell a grown up. Think about who you could talk to and draw pictures of them.

Hopscotch ◆ Looking after ourselves KS1/P1–3   PHOTOCOPIABLE PAGE   33

◆ What would you do? ◆

◆ Look at the picture. Think about what you would do if this was you.

"Give us those sweets or we'll hit you!"

◆ Talk to your friends about it and draw pictures to show what might happen.

◆ Can you help? ◆

◆ Look at this picture. The child is being bullied by others in his class.

◆ Make some suggestions for things he could do that would help him.

_____
_____
_____
_____
_____
_____
_____

Keeping safe at home

FOCUS BOOK

LOOK OUT AT HOME
by Helena Ramsay
Evans Brothers

INTENDED LEARNING

◆ To heighten the children's awareness of the hazards that exist within the home.
◆ To generate strategies for reducing the risk of accidents in the home.

Synopsis of the story

This simple non-fiction text revolves around the scenario of a family whose two-year-old cousin is coming to stay. They want to make sure that the house is a safe place for her and take precautions to ensure that she will not come to any harm. The book visits each room in the house flagging up potential sources of danger and looking at what action may be taken to prevent any accidents. All the common household hazards are covered and the book provides a good springboard for generating discussion about safety in the home. The illustrations combine drawings with photographs of a toddler which help to give the scenario meaning.

Notes for teachers

'Look out at Home' has been written in consultation with RoSPA (Royal Society for the Prevention of Accidents) and deals with all the major hazards to be encountered in the home. Every year children are killed and injured by accidents in the home; accidents which, with a little care, could have been avoided. The good thing about this text is the way in which it enables the children to think about safety issues through considering the needs of a much younger child. At some time in their career most teachers will have come face to face with the consequences of accidents in the home. By sharing this text with the children we can heighten their awareness of potentially dangerous situations and help them to take care of themselves.

Methodology

- The children may not be aware of the number of accidents that occur in the home each year so it may be worth explaining this to them and emphasising that there are things in every house that can be dangerous and hurt us. Ask: What are the things in your house that you think could be dangerous? (The children could brainstorm a list.)
- Pages 6-13 look at dangers in the kitchen. Ask: In what ways do you think the cooker could be dangerous? What other things found in the kitchen could be dangerous? Why is it important for very young children to stay away from irons? In what ways could they hurt themselves?
- Pages 14 and 15 deal with electric sockets. Ask: Why are electric sockets dangerous? Why are they especially dangerous to very young children? The children may need some clarification with regard to what can happen when things are poked into power points.
- Pages 16 and 17 deal with plastic bags. Ask: What can happen to young children if they put a plastic bag over their head? Why does this happen? This may need further explanation for some children as they may not understand the process through which suffocation can take place.
- Pages 18-21 deals with hazards associated with fires. Ask the children: Why should you never play with matches? How can fire guards help to keep us safe?
- Pages 22 and 23 deal with safety on the stairs. Ask: In what ways can we make stairs a safer place for young children?
- Pages 24 and 25 address safety in the bathroom. Ask: What things can be found in the bathroom that could be dangerous for young children?
- This is a good opportunity to discuss the various symbols on bottles of bleach and so on and to ensure that the children understand their meaning.
- Can you think of any other things you might use in the home to help keep young children safe?
- The children could look through catalogues, such as the Mothercare catalogue for items that help to keep children safe. The children may well wish to share their own experiences of accidents at home. At this point it is worth stressing that no matter how careful we are accidents can sometimes happen. This may well lead on to certain first-aid issues and how we respond in such situations.

The photocopiable activity sheets

Make the room safe The purpose of this activity is to stimulate children's thinking about dangers in the home. No writing is required.

A safe place to keep things This activity asks the children to think about safe places for keeping things that could be hazardous. They respond through drawings.

Keeping children safe This activity has a similar objective to the previous two but is intended for children who are able to write independently.

FURTHER READING

Take Care At Home by Carole Wales (Wayland)

◆ Make the room safe ◆

◆ Look carefully at this picture. Put a red ✖ by all the things that you think could be dangerous.

38   PHOTOCOPIABLE PAGE   **Hopscotch** ◆ Looking after ourselves KS1/P1–3

A safe place to keep things

◆ Draw pictures to show a safe place for each of these things.

Hopscotch ◆ Looking after ourselves KS1/P1–3   PHOTOCOPIABLE PAGE

◆ Keeping children safe ◆

◆ This little girl is going to stay with her grandparents.

◆ Make a list of all the things the grandparents will need to do to make the room safe for their grandchild.

_____
_____
_____
_____
_____
_____

Road safety

FOCUS BOOK

TAKE CARE ON THE ROAD
by Carole Wale
Wayland

INTENDED LEARNING

◆ To encourage the children to think about how accidents on the road can be avoided. To give them information and strategies that will help them develop safety skills and good road safety habits.

Synopsis of the text

'Take Care On The Road' is a non-fiction text that deals with most safety issues that would be encountered in a busy built-up area. It is attractively illustrated with photographs and features an appealing cartoon cat who gives road safety guidance. The photographs show adults and children from a variety of cultures and gender issues are sensitively dealt with.

The aim of this book is to encourage young children to play an active role in their own safety. It contains notes for parents and teachers. The author, Carole Wale, produces safety education resources for children of all ages and is Editor of RoSPA's Safety Education journal.

Notes for teachers

This book is from Wayland's 'Take Care' series and has an easy-to-read text that can also provide valuable support with literacy work. Understandably, the text works from the assumption that all child pedestrians will be accompanied by an adult, which, as we are all aware, is sometimes not the case. The real challenge for us as teachers is in enabling children to understand and internalise the information to the extent that they are able to keep themselves safe. This text deals with situations that are familiar to children and provides a good vehicle through which we can work towards this aim. In the key questions we will address the issue of what might help ensure children's safety when alone near busy roads.

Methodology

◆ The photographs in this book are lively and immediate and generally provoke an equally lively response from the children. They enjoy making comparisons between the familiar situations presented and their own experiences.

◆ Ask the children: Why is it important to hold an adult's hand when you are out and about? How would you keep yourself safe if you were by yourself in a busy street? What are the important things to think about when walking along a pavement?

◆ Pages 12-17 explain why it is important to STOP, LOOK and LISTEN. Ask the children the following questions:
  - Why is it so important to stop at the kerb before crossing the road?
  - Once you have stopped at the kerb what things do you look for?
  - What things do you listen for?
  - What do you have to know and remember when using a pelican crossing?
  - How can pedestrians help road users to see them more clearly, especially if it is dark and gloomy?
  - Who are the people that can help us when we need to cross a busy street?

◆ The book tells us that subways, pelican crossings, zebra crossings and footbridges are good places to cross the road. What is it about these places that makes them safe?

◆ Pages 26 and 27 deal with learning to cycle. Ask the children:
  - What are the things you have found difficult about learning to ride a bicycle?
  - Why is it important to have the seat at the right height?
  - Why is it important to practise in a safe place?
  - What sort of things can you wear to help keep you safe when riding a bicycle?
  - Why is it dangerous to play on pavements or near to roads?
  - Can you think of some safe places to play?
  - Do you think the places where you play are safe?

◆ Other questions to ask are: What sort of dangers could you meet on a quiet road? What safety rules should you remember when travelling by car? What are the important safety rules when travelling by bus?

The photocopiable activity sheets

Safe places to play This activity asks the children to think about safe places to play. They respond by drawing themselves into the pictures.

Keeping safe near roads The objective for this activity is the same as for the previous one. The children will need to discuss alternatives and then respond by drawing pictures.

Josie's journey This sheet asks the children to think about the variety of situations that might be encountered on a journey. It is intended for independent writers.

Safe places to play

◆ Look at the pictures and think where it would be safe to play. Draw yourself and your friends in the pictures where it is safe.

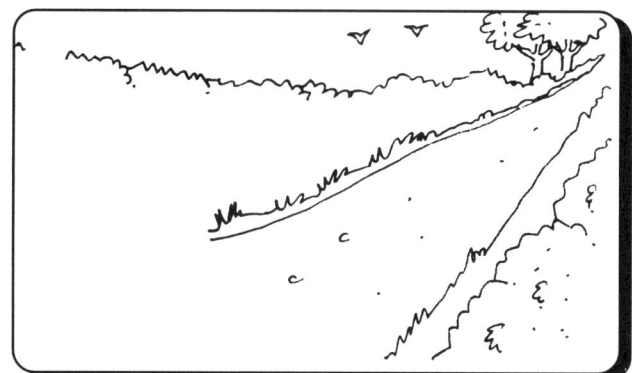

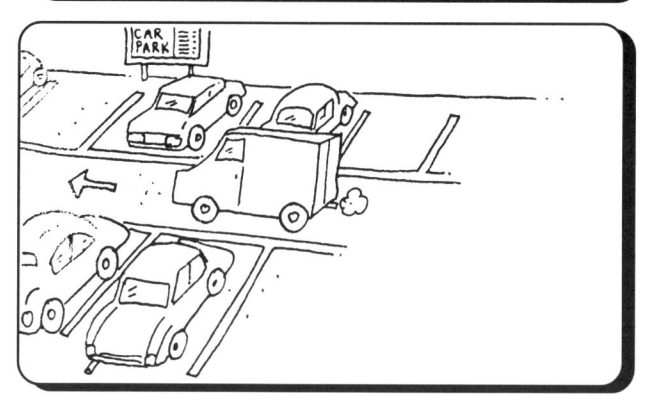

Hopscotch ◆ Looking after ourselves KS1/P1–3   PHOTOCOPIABLE PAGE

Keeping safe near roads

◆ These children are in danger. Draw pictures to show how they could keep themselves safe.

◆ Josie's journey ◆

◆ Underneath each picture write the things Josie needs to know in order to keep safe on the road.

_____
_____
_____

_____
_____
_____

_____
_____
_____

_____
_____
_____

Hopscotch ◆ Looking after ourselves KS1/P1–3   PHOTOCOPIABLE PAGE   45

Charlie and the bag

◆ Charlie found a bag of drugs. Draw and write.

1. What was in the bag?

2. Who dropped it?

3. What would you do with it?

4. Can drugs be good for you? If so, when?

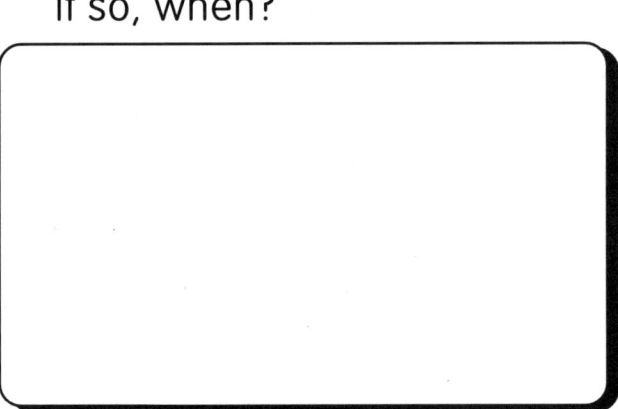

5. Can drugs be bad for you? If so, when?

◆ Looking after ourselves ◆

◆ Under each picture write a sentence to tell these children how they can take care of themselves.

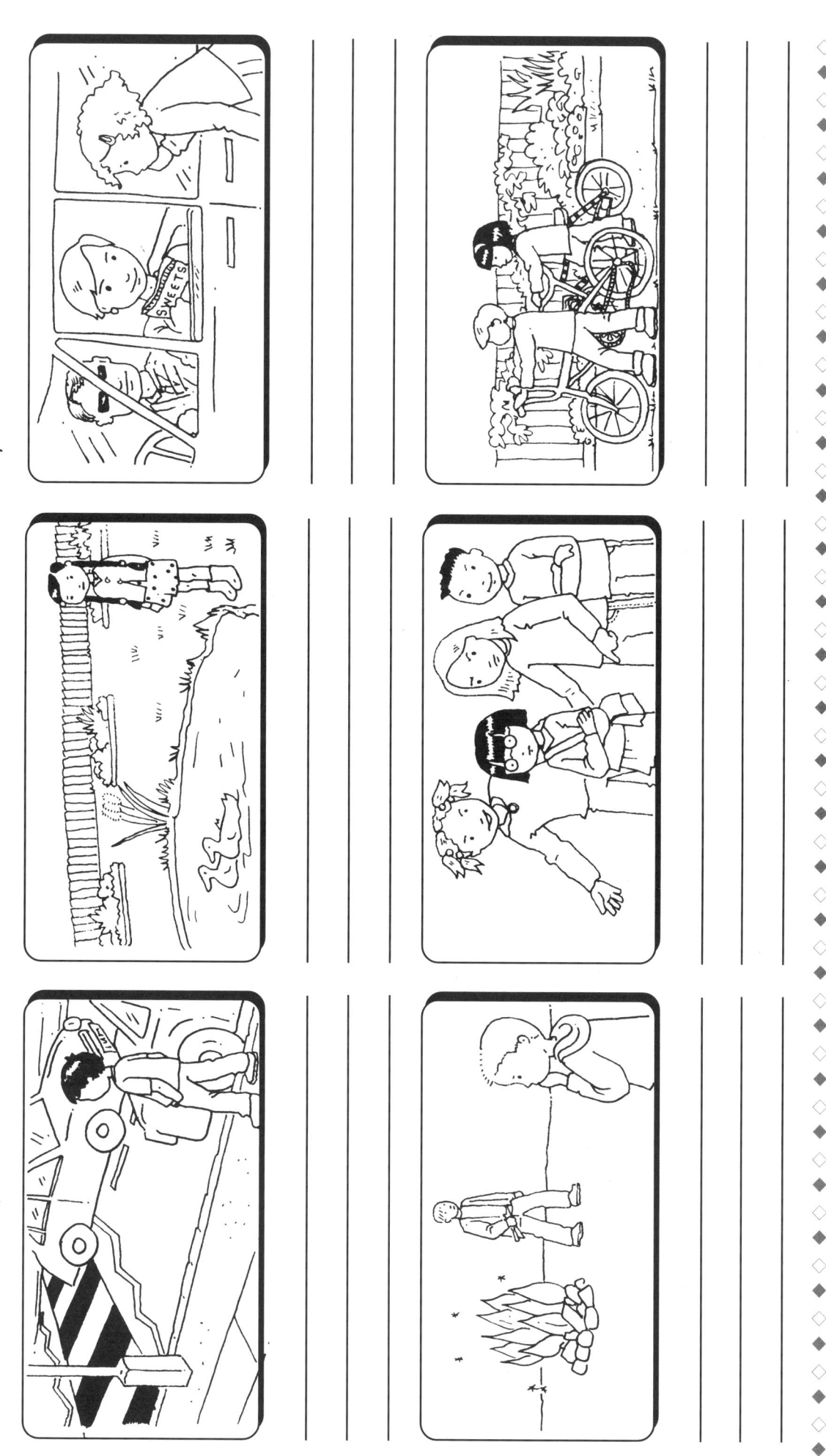

Hopscotch ◆ Looking after ourselves KS1/P1–3   PHOTOCOPIABLE PAGE   47